CONTENTS

FROM OVEN TO TABLE

*T*he aroma of pizza baking is one of the
most appetizing scents imaginable; the mere
sight of a well-endowed pizza being carried
from oven to table promises good food
and good times. Pizza is both party fare and
comfort food, as festive and fun as it is soothing
and satisfying. And, as you'll discover in
Pizza Primer, it's fun, economical, and
simple to make at home.

THE HOME PIZZERIA

Making pizza at home is no more difficult than baking bread and requires no special equipment other than a hot oven. "Hot" means an oven that's been preheated to 450°F (230°C). If you prefer the crust quite crisp, the oven should be set at 475°F (235°C); some experts like an even hotter oven.

EQUIPMENT AND TOOLS

Pizza has been made by hand for centuries, and many purists insist this is still the only proper way to make it. But although preparing dough by hand can be satisfying and even fun, having the right equipment and tools streamlines the process and can add to the pleasures of the home pizzeria. Before using any food processor, kitchen mixer, automatic breadmaker, or any other appliance, be sure to consult the owner's manual that came with the machine.

Food processor Using a food processor, you can blend the dry ingredients for pizza dough in about a minute and then complete the kneading by hand. If your processor is designed to handle heavy doughs, you can use the machine to knead the dough (see page 20).

Heavy-duty mixer You can use almost any kitchen mixer to blend the dry ingredients for pizza dough; however, only a heavy-duty mixer fitted with a dough hook has a sufficiently powerful motor to mix and knead yeast doughs (see page 17).

Automatic breadmaker An automatic breadmaker represents the ultimate in convenience: With one of these machines you simply pour in the ingredients and set the machine for the dough cycle. The pizza dough is then automatically mixed, kneaded, and raised in a thermostatically controlled environment. Although there are a number of different brands and models on the market, almost all of them prepare pizza dough in the same way (see page 21).

Baker's peel One of the most useful tools in a pizza parlor is the baker's peel, a large paddle made of smooth basswood used to transport pizzas to and from the ovens. If the surface of the peel is sprinkled with cornmeal to prevent sticking, the pizza dough can be allowed to rise and the crust shaped and topped directly on the peel. After use, the peel should be wiped with a damp cloth and any bits of food scraped off. Washing the peel under running water or soaking it will cause the wood to warp and split.

Baking stone The ovens in most traditional pizzerias have porous brick or stone walls that absorb moisture from the dough and distribute the heat efficiently, producing a crisp crust. A baking stone made of unglazed high-fired stoneware helps produce similar results in a home oven. The stone is placed on the lowest rack and preheats along with the oven. A baker's peel is used to slide the uncooked pizza onto the stone in the oven (see page 6). After the pizza has baked and been removed from the oven, the stone remains in the oven to cool and can be stored there permanently.

Pizza pans With bakeware as in everything else, the best quality usually ends up costing the least in the long run. Heavy-gauge aluminum and black steel are good choices for pizza pans, although some cooks prefer air-cushioned bakeware with a layer of air sandwiched between two sheets of aluminum to help distribute heat evenly. Also popular are perforated pans that allow moisture to escape and heat to penetrate, ensuring a crisp crust. Aficionados of Chicago-style pizza will want their own authentic steel deep-dish pan with high sides, just like the ones pizza parlors use. Some pans are even designed with special hand grips for rushing the pizza from oven to table.

With use, aluminum bakeware will darken and become "seasoned," which improves its heat conductivity and produces an even better crust. Both black steel and darkened aluminum pans should be washed (not scrubbed) with warm sudsy water, rinsed, and wiped dry. Scrubbing will wear away the seasoning on the pans and cause the dough to stick.

The deep-dish pizzas in this book require a pan about 15 inches (37.5 cm) in diameter and 2 inches (5 cm) deep. Almost all the other recipes in this book call for a 16-inch (40-cm) pan, but you can shape the dough into four 8-inch (20-cm) pizzas if your oven is too narrow to accommodate the larger size of pan.

Pizza wheel This rolling blade is useful for trimming pizza dough, slicing baked pizza, or for cutting fresh pasta, pastry, or cookie dough. When selecting a pizza wheel, be sure the blade turns freely; the best designs have a guard to protect the fingers.

PIZZA PROVISIONS

Making pizza at home means always being able to have your favorite pizza made precisely the way you like it, with just the right crust and toppings. With a little advance preparation and a few well-chosen provisions from your cupboard and refrigerator or freezer, you can have five-star pizza made from scratch for far less than you'd pay for a frozen one from the store.

Ingredients for pizza dough You probably already have on hand the basic ingredients for most of the pizza doughs presented in this book: flour, yeast, salt, oil, and honey or sugar.

Most of the recipes for pizza dough in this book call for unbleached flour or a mixture of unbleached and whole wheat flour or semolina. A coarsely ground, unbleached flour made from durum wheat, semolina produces a sturdy dough that yields a crisp crust with a chewy interior. Replacing part of the unbleached flour with cornmeal, rolled oats, rye or soy flour, or other ingredients can produce a crust with distinctive texture and flavor but will slow the rising of the dough.

When you purchase yeast, check the label on the foil packet or jar to be sure the expiration date has not passed. Old yeast cultures may be too weak to raise dough properly. Buy only as much yeast as you can use before the expiration date passes. Dry yeast (regular or fast-rising) can be stored in a cupboard; cake (compressed) yeast is highly perishable and should be refrigerated.

Besides enhancing flavor, the use of salt, oil, and honey, sugar, or other sweeteners contributes to the proper rising of the dough. Salt helps control the rate of fermentation, while a light coating of

oil keeps the surface of the dough pliable so that it can expand
easily. A small amount of honey or sugar supports the growth of
the yeast, although too much can slow the rate.

Raising the dough   Yeast doughs rise as a result of fermentation
produced by yeast cultures. The fermentation releases carbon
dioxide into the dough, causing it to expand. The optimum
temperature for triggering fermentation varies according to the
type of yeast used. Cake yeast and active dry yeast are mixed with
water or other liquid heated to about 105°F (41°C). Fast-rising
active dry yeast requires a slightly higher temperature—about
120°F (49°C). This special strain of fast-acting yeast, which is
usually blended with dry ingredients before being mixed with very
warm liquid, can shorten rising times by half.

Some cooks prefer to "proof" yeast, or test it for potency, before
proceeding with a yeast dough recipe: The yeast is stirred into
warm water to activate it; if the mixture fails to foam after 5
minutes, the yeast cultures are considered too weak to raise dough
properly. Proofing is not generally necessary if you are careful to
use yeast before the date on the package label has expired.

Yeast dough rises best under moist, warm conditions. The ideal temperature for rising is about 80°F to 85°F (27°C to 29°C). If the room temperature is too cold for proper rising, you can set the dough to rise in a gas oven warmed by a pilot light or in an electric oven that has been heated to 200°F (95°C) for 1 minute, then turned off. Add moisture by placing the bowl of dough over (not in) a pan of very warm water. Another way to create a moist, warm environment is with a microwave oven: Microwave 2 cups (500 ml) of water until the water boils and then turn off the power, set the dough in the microwave oven, and close the door. You can even let pizza dough rise in the refrigerator for several hours, overnight, or for up to 2 days. Simply remove the raised dough, punch it down (see page 16) and let it warm to room temperature before shaping, topping, and baking.

Freezing unbaked pizza crust Freezing an unbaked pizza crust allows you to do the preparation and clean-up when it's most convenient for you, then top and bake the pizza when you want to serve it. This method is especially valuable when you're preparing pizza for a crowd (see page 84). Let the dough rise as usual, then punch down, roll out, and shape into a crust of the desired size (see page 16). Coat the crust lightly with oil and place in a pizza pan lined with heavy-duty aluminum foil topped with plastic wrap. Fold additional plastic wrap loosely over the top and freeze the crust until it is solid. Remove the frozen crust from the pan and rewrap tightly, molding the foil to eliminate air pockets. Label and date the package and then return it to the freezer for no more than two weeks.

To defrost, remove the frozen crust from its wrappings. Place it in the pizza pan in which it was frozen and cover loosely with a damp towel or plastic wrap. Let stand in a warm place until doubled in bulk, from 1½ to 4 hours, depending upon the room temperature and the diameter and thickness of the crust. Add toppings and bake as you would any other pizza crust.

Ingredients for sauces and toppings Pizza is extraordinarily versatile, accepting an almost endless variety of sauces and toppings. Once you've mastered the basic pizza doughs (see pages 14–23), let your imagination and whatever is available at the

market drive the selection of toppings to adorn your pizzas. Don't forget that choice leftovers from your refrigerator can come to life again in a sauce or topping for a well-designed pizza. Remember that the quality of the ingredients you choose is paramount. For specific suggestions, see pages 24–33.

THE WORLD OF PIZZA

Pizza assumes many different guises, all of them delightful. Not all of them look like a standard pizza, even though they may be close relatives. The difference is one of form, rather than nature, since the ingredients are essentially the same. Focaccia, pizzette, and other flatbreads are the ancestors of classic Neapolitan pizza (see pages 58–63). Another of pizza's relatives is calzone, a plump turnover shaped like a half moon and bulging with a pizza-style filling (see pages 66–69). From traditional Italian and Italian-American pizzas to contemporary specialties that aren't the least bit Italian, the world of pizza offers something for everyone. Once you've mastered the basics presented in *Pizza Primer*, let your own good taste guide you in creating a variety of custom-designed pizzas that will all become your favorites.

RECIPES AND TECHNIQUES FOR THE HOME PIZZERIA

*T*he beauty of pizza is its versatility.
Once you master the basic recipes
and techniques, you can use your imagination
(and whatever's available in the refrigerator and
pantry) to turn out an almost unlimited number
of pizza varieties. The 50 recipes that
follow merely hint at the enormous range of
traditional pizza specialties and contemporary
classics you can create at home.

DOUGHS FOR PIZZA CRUSTS

Making pizza dough from scratch gives you complete control over the flavor and texture of the very foundation of every good pizza—the crust. From a sturdy hand-kneaded Neapolitan dough to one that practically makes itself in an automatic breadmaker, this section presents a collection of basic doughs and crusts with which you can build an impressive pizza repertoire.

BASIC PIZZA DOUGH

A simple, straightforward dough enriched with oil, this one is ready to use in a little more than an hour. For a firm, elastic dough that yields a crisp, finely textured crust, replace up to half the unbleached flour with semolina, a high-protein flour ground from hard durum wheat.

½ pkg (1½ tsp)	active dry yeast	½ pkg (1½ tsp)
¾ cup	warm water (about 105°F or 41°C)	175 ml
2 tbl	olive oil	2 tbl
about 2½ cups	unbleached flour	about 600 ml
1 tsp	salt	1 tsp
as needed	oil, for bowl	as needed

1. In a small bowl dissolve yeast in the warm water and let stand 5 minutes. Stir in olive oil. In a large bowl combine flour and salt. Add yeast mixture and stir until dough just barely holds together.

2. Turn dough out on a lightly floured surface and knead until smooth and silky, adding a little more flour if dough seems sticky. Put dough in an oiled bowl and turn to coat surface with oil. Cover bowl with plastic wrap and let rise in a warm place until doubled in bulk (about 1 hour).

3. Punch dough down and shape according to instructions in Step 3 on page 16.

Makes one 16-inch (40-cm) pizza crust.

KNEADING AND SHAPING PIZZA DOUGH

Transforming a rather amorphous mass of flour and liquid into a smooth, springy dough that yields a delicious pizza crust begins with proper kneading and shaping. After mixing your favorite dough recipe by hand, in a mixer, or in a food processor, follow the instructions given below. For instructions on kneading dough in an automatic breadmaker, see page 21.

2. After dough has risen until doubled in bulk, punch it down, using your fist in a straight-down motion.

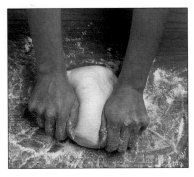

1. Place dough on a lightly floured surface and knead until it is smooth and silky, adding more flour if necessary.

3. To shape into pizza crust, on lightly floured surface, roll dough out about ¼ inch (.6 cm) thick, to desired size. Place on baker's peel or oiled pizza pan dusted with cornmeal.

WHOLE WHEAT PIZZA DOUGH

Whole wheat flour produces a dense, chewy crust with a hearty, satisfying flavor. Doughs containing whole wheat tend to rise more slowly than those made with unbleached flour, but using fast-rising active dry yeast reduces the rising time by about half (see page 9). This recipe calls for a heavy-duty electric mixer, but you can mix the dough by hand.

about 2 cups	unbleached flour	about 500 ml
½ cup	whole wheat flour	125 ml
1 pkg (1 tbl)	fast-rising active dry yeast	1 pkg (1 tbl)
½ tsp	salt	½ tsp
1 cup	very warm water (about 120°F or 49°C)	250 ml
1 tsp	honey	1 tsp
2 tsp	olive oil	2 tsp
as needed	oil, for bowl	as needed

1. In large bowl of heavy-duty electric mixer, combine 1⅔ cups (400 ml) of the unbleached flour, the whole wheat flour, yeast, and salt. Stir to blend dry ingredients thoroughly.

2. In a small bowl combine water, honey, and oil; stir to blend well. Add water mixture to flour mixture. Mix to blend, then beat at medium speed until smooth and elastic (about 5 minutes). Stir in about ⅓ cup (85 ml) more unbleached flour to make a soft dough.

3. Turn dough out onto a well-floured board or pastry cloth. Knead until dough is smooth and elastic (5–10 minutes), adding just enough unbleached flour (up to ⅓ cup or 85 ml) to prevent dough from being sticky.

4. Place dough in an oiled bowl and turn to coat evenly. Cover with plastic wrap and let rise in a warm place until doubled in bulk (30–40 minutes).

5. Punch dough down, cover with inverted bowl, and let rest for 10 minutes. Shape according to instructions in Step 3 on page 16.

Makes one 16-inch (40-cm) pizza crust.

NEAPOLITAN PIZZA DOUGH

This classic Neapolitan pizza dough yields a dry crisp crust that can support a moist topping, such as fresh clams (see page 35). The recipe contains no oil other than what is used for oiling the bowl and the dough prior to rising. Allowing the dough to rise twice produces a pleasing, yeasty flavor.

1 pkg (1 tbl)	dry yeast	1 pkg (1 tbl)
¾ cup	warm water (about 105°F or 41°C)	175 ml
about 2½ cups	unbleached flour	about 600 ml
½ tsp	salt	½ tsp
as needed	oil, for bowl	as needed

1. In a medium bowl dissolve yeast in the water. Add 1¼ cups (300 ml) of the flour and mix well to make a sponge, or a soft batter-like dough. Cover with plastic wrap and let rise 45 minutes.

2. In a large bowl, combine remaining flour and the salt. Add risen sponge and mix well. Turn out onto a lightly floured surface and knead until smooth and silky (about 5 minutes), adding flour as necessary. Put dough in an oiled bowl and turn to coat evenly. Cover and let rise 2 hours.

3. Punch dough down and shape according to instructions in Step 3 on page 16.

Makes one 16-inch (40-cm) pizza crust.

FOOD PROCESSOR PIZZA DOUGH

A food processor fitted with a steel blade can mix pizza dough in seconds. If your food processor is powerful enough to handle heavy yeast doughs without damaging the motor, you can also use it to knead the dough (consult the manufacturer's instructions to be sure). If necessary, mix the ingredients in the food processor and complete the kneading by hand (see page 16).

about 2½ cups	unbleached flour	about 600 ml
1 pkg (1 tbl)	fast-rising active dry yeast	1 pkg (1 tbl)
½ tsp	salt	½ tsp
1 cup	very warm water (about 120°F or 49°C)	250 ml
1 tsp	honey	1 tsp
2 tsp	olive oil	2 tsp
as needed	oil, for bowl	as needed

1. In work bowl of food processor fitted with a steel blade, mix flour, yeast, and salt. Combine the water, honey, and olive oil in a measuring cup. With processor running, pour water mixture through feed tube in a steady stream, adjusting the amount poured so flour can absorb it. Turn processor off when dough gathers into clumps and before it forms a smooth ball. Do not overprocess. Dough should feel a little sticky. If it is too soft, add more flour, 1 tablespoon at a time, until dough has a firm consistency.

2. Knead by processing for an additional 45 seconds or knead by hand until dough is smooth and silky. Shape into a ball.

3. Place dough in an oiled bowl and turn to coat evenly. Cover with plastic wrap and let rise in a warm place until dough is doubled in bulk (30–40 minutes).

4. Punch dough down, cover with inverted bowl, and let rest for 10 minutes. Shape according to instructions in Step 3 on page 16.

Makes one 16-inch (40-cm) pizza crust.

BREADMAKER PIZZA DOUGH

Making pizza dough in an automatic breadmaker takes almost no effort. You simply place the ingredients in the bread pan that comes with the machine, and the dough is automatically mixed, kneaded, and raised at a controlled temperature. When the timer on the machine indicates that the cycle is complete (after about an hour or so), you remove the dough, shape it into a crust, and top and bake it in the oven as you would any pizza. For specific instructions on the order of ingredients and setting the machine for mixing and raising pizza dough, consult the owner's manual that came with your breadmaker. The semolina flour produces a chewy crust with a crisp exterior.

¾ cup	water	175 ml
⅓ cup	olive oil	85 ml
1¼ cups	semolina flour	300 ml
1¼ cups	unbleached flour	300 ml
½ tsp	salt	½ tsp
½ pkg (1½ tsp)	yeast	½ pkg (1½ tsp)

1. Place all ingredients in pan of breadmaker in the order given (follow manufacturer's instructions). Put pan in breadmaker and select setting for mixing dough.

2. When dough cycle is complete, remove dough from breadmaker pan. Shape according to instructions in Step 3 on page 16 or place dough in a plastic bag and refrigerate for up to two days in the refrigerator before shaping.

Makes one 16-inch (40-cm) pizza crust.

DEEP-DISH PIZZA DOUGH

Traditional deep-dish (Chicago-style) pizzas are baked in a special high-sided pan that resembles an oversized cake pan. This recipe makes enough dough to line a pan about 15 inches (37.5 cm) in diameter and 2 inches (5 cm) deep. If you prefer a crust that is crisp on the outside, with a chewy interior, replace up to half of the unbleached flour with semolina (see page 8).

about 3 cups	unbleached flour	about 700 ml
1 pkg (1 tbl)	fast-rising active dry yeast	1 pkg (1 tbl)
¾ tsp	salt	¾ tsp
1¼ cups	very warm water (about 120°F or 49°C)	300 ml
2 tsp	honey	2 tsp
1 tbl	olive oil	1 tbl
as needed	oil, for bowl	as needed

1. In large bowl combine 2½ cups (600 ml) of the flour, yeast, and salt. Stir to blend dry ingredients thoroughly. In a small bowl combine water, honey, and oil; stir to blend well.

2. Add water mixture to flour mixture. Mix to blend, then beat by hand or with an electric mixer set at medium speed until smooth and elastic (about 5 minutes). Stir in about ½ cup (125 ml) more flour to make a soft dough.

3. Turn dough out onto a floured board or pastry cloth. Knead until dough is smooth and satiny (8–10 minutes), adding more flour if dough is sticky.

4. Place dough in an oiled bowl and turn to coat evenly. Cover with plastic wrap and let rise in a warm place until doubled in bulk (30–40 minutes).

5. Punch dough down, cover with inverted bowl, and let rest for 10 minutes. Shape according to instructions in Step 3 on page 16.

Makes one 15-inch (37.5-cm) deep-dish pizza crust.

SAUCES AND TOPPINGS FOR PIZZA

Sauces and toppings are the crowning glory of any pizza. By learning to prepare the collection of flavorful sauces in this section, you'll never again have to rely on commercial concoctions of mediocre ingredients. And by learning to select and combine ingredients for a variety of toppings, you'll experience the satisfaction of preparing one great pizza after another, each made exactly as you like it.

BASIC TOMATO PIZZA SAUCE

The secret to the flavor of this quick, low-fat sauce, which uses very little oil, is steeping the basil and oregano in wine before cooking. This simple step draws out the flavor of the herbs, creating a sauce that tastes as if it had been cooking for hours. This recipe calls for fresh tomatoes, but you can also use imported canned tomatoes.

1½ tbl	minced fresh basil	1½ tbl
½ tsp	dried oregano	½ tsp
1½ tbl	white wine	1½ tbl
¼ cup	grated onion	60 ml
1 tsp	minced garlic	1 tsp
1 tsp	olive oil	1 tsp
1½ cups	peeled, seeded, and chopped tomatoes (see page 28)	350 ml
1½ tsp	tomato paste	1½ tsp

1. In a small bowl steep basil and oregano in white wine for 10 minutes.

2. In a skillet over medium-high heat, sauté onion and garlic in olive oil for 5 minutes, stirring frequently. Add tomatoes and tomato paste, then steeped herbs and wine. Cover, reduce heat, and simmer 15 minutes.

3. Remove sauce from heat and purée in a blender or food processor.

Makes about 1½ cups (350 ml).

Spicy Pizza Sauce

A thick hearty sauce like this one is ideal for Chicago-Style pizza (see pages 75 and 76.) You can substitute imported canned tomatoes for the fresh ones.

1 tbl	olive oil	1 tbl
½	onion, finely chopped	½
½ cup	thinly sliced mushrooms	125 ml
1 clove	garlic, minced	1 clove
1½ cups	peeled, seeded, and chopped tomatoes (see page 28)	1½ cups
1½ tbl	tomato paste	1½ tbl
pinch each	salt, pepper, and dried oregano	pinch each
1 tbl	chopped fresh basil	1 tbl

1. In a saucepan heat oil over medium heat; add onion and mushrooms. Cook, stirring often, until onion is soft and mushrooms brown lightly. Mix in garlic, tomatoes with their juice, tomato paste, salt, pepper, oregano, and basil. Bring to a boil, cover, reduce heat, and simmer for 20 minutes.

2. Uncover, increase heat until sauce simmers gently, and continue cooking until sauce is thickened and reduced to about 1½ cups (300 ml) (12–15 minutes).

Makes about 1½ cups (300 ml).

PREPARING TOMATOES

When you select fresh tomatoes for topping a pizza or making pizza sauce, choose varieties that have a high proportion of meat to seeds and juice; these are often labeled as plum, pear, or paste tomatoes in the markets and in garden seed catalogues. Select tomatoes that are fragrant and fully ripe, and keep them out of the refrigerator if you want to maintain peak flavor.

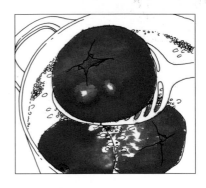

2. Put the tomatoes in a pan containing enough boiling water to cover them and boil for 15 seconds. Remove them with a slotted spoon and put them in a bowl of cold water. Leave for a few seconds.

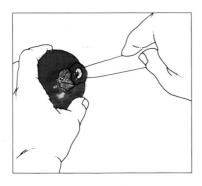

1. Use a paring knife to core the tomatoes. Turn tomatoes over and slit the skin in an X-shaped cut.

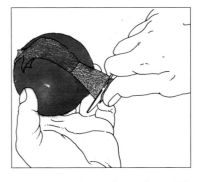

3. Remove them from the cold water and use a paring knife to pull off the skins. Halve the tomatoes horizontally with a chopping knife. Hold each half over a bowl, cut side down, and squeeze to remove the seeds. Chop the tomatoes into small pieces.

Pesto Pizza Sauce

The pungent, licorice-like aroma and flavor of basil make a mouth-watering tomato-less sauce. In the summer farmer's markets and roadside stands in many areas offer several different varieties of basil that can produce an assortment of pestos, each with its own distinctive flavor and hue. In the winter, try substituting fresh spinach for the basil. Pesto also marries nicely with pasta, rice, or even fresh Italian or French bread.

2 cups	fresh basil leaves, loosely packed	500 ml
¼ cup	olive oil	60 ml
2 tbl	pine nuts, toasted	2 tbl
2 cloves	garlic, minced	2 cloves
½ tsp	salt	½ tsp
⅓ cup	freshly grated Parmesan cheese	85 ml
⅓ cup	freshly grated Romano cheese	85 ml

1. Put basil, olive oil, pine nuts, garlic, and salt in a blender or food processor. Blend or process until smooth.

2. Transfer to a bowl and stir in Parmesan and Romano cheeses.

Makes about 1 cup (250 ml).

Preparing Garlic

Choose fresh whole garlic heads that look plump and feel firm. Avoid heads that are withered or have bruised or darkened cloves. Store in a cool, dry, dark place with good air circulation. Try to leave the heads whole until you are ready to use them; cloves that have been separated from the head dry out rapidly and should be used as soon as possible.

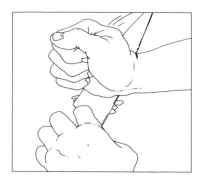

2. Return garlic to board and position knife above it as in step 1. Hit blade vigorously with side of fist to crush the garlic.

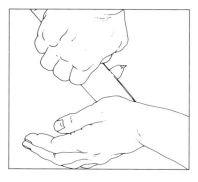

1. Put garlic clove on a board. Hold flat side of a large knife just above it. Lightly pound knife, hitting the garlic and loosening its skin. Pull skin off, cutting if necessary.

3. To chop the garlic, cut it several times in one direction. Then slice it against the direction of the first cuts. To mince the garlic, continue chopping until very finely minced.

GARLIC-OREGANO PIZZA SAUCE

Choose young, unsprouted garlic, virgin olive oil, and fresh oregano for the best results. This sauce is delectable in its simplicity.

6 cloves	young garlic, minced very fine (see page 30)	6 cloves
½ cup	olive oil	125 ml
½ cup	dry white wine	125 ml
2 tbl	chopped fresh oregano	2 tbl
to taste	salt and frshly ground black pepper	to taste
to taste	freshly grated Parmesan cheese	to taste

1. In a small saucepan over low heat, cook garlic, ¼ cup (60 ml) of the olive oil, and wine until garlic is very soft (about 45 minutes). The mixture will have the consistency of a rough paste.

2. Spread the paste on the pizza dough. Drizzle with remaining olive oil and sprinkle with oregano. Season with salt, pepper, and Parmesan cheese.

Makes about 1 cup (250 ml).

TOPPINGS WITH PIZZAZZ

Toppings put the pizzazz into pizza. Simple or elaborate, traditional or cutting-edge, it's toppings that give pizzas their distinctive identities, if not their names. A dusting of tangy Parmesan over spicy salami slices and tomato sauce; heaps of sautéed onions, peppers, and mushrooms flecked with fresh herbs; smoky provolone dotted with pepperoni; bits of smoked turkey brushed with barbecue sauce and topped with shreds of Monterey jack; chunks of ham and pineapple surrounded by creamy mozzarella; a layer of chunky salsa topped with asadero cheese and sprinkled with chopped cilantro; sharp cheddar with strips of thinly sliced roast beef—the list of likely (and unlikely) combinations is endless. When it comes to combining different toppings, the rules are few:

- *Make certain that everything you select to top your pizza is of the best quality; a modest sprinkling of a fine-quality imported cheese or a light drizzle of the best virgin olive oil you can afford is a better value in the long run than a larger quantity of a mediocre product.*

- *Use good judgment about the number of toppings you combine. More is not always better!*

TRADITIONAL PIZZAS AND VARIATIONS

Originating most likely in Naples as a simple flatbread, what we think of as "pizza" is only one member of a family of traditional Italian bread-based foods that serve as plate and meal in one. As you'll discover in this section of traditional recipes ranging from conventional Neapolitan versions to calzone and other classic variations, few Italian dishes are as familiar to Americans as pizza, or as irresistible.

Pizza alle Vongole

Rubbery clams and overcooked tomato sauce are the norm on many restaurant clam pizzas. You can make a far better version at home with fresh, chopped tomatoes and freshly steamed clams. To keep the clams ("vongole" in Italian) from toughening, add them just as the pizza comes out of the oven.

1¼ cups	peeled, seeded, and chopped tomatoes (see page 28)	300 ml
4 tbl	olive oil	4 tbl
1 tbl	minced fresh oregano	1 tbl
1 recipe	Neapolitan Pizza Dough (see page 18)	1 recipe
1 tbl	minced garlic	1 tbl
½ cup	dry white wine	125 ml
1¾ lb	small clams	800 g
1 tbl	coarsely chopped Italian parsley	1 tbl

1. Preheat oven to 475°F (240°C). In a small bowl, combine tomatoes, 2 tablespoons of the olive oil, and oregano; let stand 15 minutes.

2. Shape pizza dough according to instructions in Step 3 on page 16. Brush dough with 2 tablespoons of the liquid from the tomatoes. Spoon tomatoes over dough. Bake until well-browned and puffy (about 18 minutes). Remove from oven and set aside.

3. While pizza is baking, heat remaining oil over moderately low heat in skillet large enough to hold all the clams. Add garlic and sauté until fragrant but not browned (about 2 minutes). Add wine, raise heat to high, and bring to a boil. Add clams, cover, and steam until they open (about 3–5 minutes), shaking skillet occasionally and removing any clams that have opened. Discard any clams that haven't opened after 5 minutes.

4. Remove clams from shells and discard shells. Return clams to skillet. Add parsley and remove from heat. Scatter clams over the baked pizza and serve hot.

Makes one 16-inch (40-cm) pizza.

Pizza Caponata

Eggplant makes an uncommonly tasty pizza topping.

1 medium	eggplant, unpeeled	1 medium
as needed	olive oil	as needed
2	onions, thinly sliced	2
½ cup	celery, sliced ¼-inch (.6-cm) thick	125 ml
½ cup	tomato purée	125 ml
3 tbl	minced garlic	3 tbl
2 tbl	pine nuts, toasted	2 tbl
2 tbl	sugar	2 tbl
¼ cup	red wine vinegar	60 ml
to taste	salt and pepper	to taste
½ cup	minced Italian parsley	125 ml
½ cup	chopped black olives	125 ml
1 recipe	pizza dough (see pages 15–21)	1 recipe
½ cup	grated Parmesan cheese	125 ml

1. Preheat oven to 450°F (230°C). Cut eggplant into ¾-inch (1.9-cm) cubes. In a large sauté pan over moderately high heat, heat 4 tablespoons of the oil. Add the eggplant and sauté until lightly browned and softened. Transfer eggplant to paper towels to drain.

2. In the same skillet over moderate heat, sauté onions in 2 tablespoons oil until soft but not browned. Add celery, tomato purée, and garlic; simmer 10 minutes.

3. Add toasted pine nuts to tomato mixture along with sugar, vinegar, salt, pepper, and parsley. Add eggplant and simmer 15 minutes. Remove from heat and stir in olives.

4. Shape pizza dough according to instructions in Step 3 on page 16. Top dough with eggplant mixture. Drizzle with a little more olive oil; sprinkle with Parmesan cheese. Bake until well-browned (about 20 minutes). Serve hot.

Makes one 16-inch (40-cm) pizza.

Pizza Rossa

*Sun-dried tomatoes have a sweet intensity that's almost candy-like.
Just a few, cut in strips, will enrich and enliven a topping with fresh
tomatoes. Add some sweet, height-of-summer red bell peppers and you
have a brassy, bright-red (rossa) topping for a warm-weather pizza.*

as needed	olive oil	as needed
1½ tbl	minced garlic	1½ tbl
1¼ cups	peeled, seeded, and chopped tomatoes (see page 28)	300 ml
1½ tbl	chopped fresh basil	1½ tbl
1 recipe	Neapolitan Pizza Dough (see page 18)	1 recipe
2	red bell peppers, roasted (see page 45)	2
1½ tbl	bottled sun-dried tomatoes, sliced	1½ tbl
1 tbl	oil from sun-dried tomatoes	1 tbl
1½ tbl	coarsely grated Parmesan cheese	1½ tbl

1. In a large skillet heat olive oil over moderately low heat. Add
   garlic and sauté gently until fragrant but not browned (about
   3 minutes). Add fresh tomatoes and basil; stir to mix and
   remove from heat.

2. Preheat oven to 475°F (240°C). Shape pizza dough according
   to instructions in Step 3 on page 16. Brush dough lightly with
   olive oil. Spoon fresh tomato mixture over dough and top with
   roasted red peppers. Garnish with sun-dried tomatoes. Drizzle
   with oil from sun-dried tomatoes and dust with Parmesan
   cheese. Bake until browned and bubbly (about 18 minutes).
   Serve hot.

Makes one 16-inch (40-cm) pizza.

Pizza al Pesto

The brilliant green of the pesto on this pizza is the perfect counterpoint to all-red Pizza Rossa (see photo on page 39).

1 recipe	Neapolitan Pizza Dough (see page 18)	1 recipe
1 cup	grated mozzarella cheese	250 ml
1 recipe	Pesto Pizza Sauce (see page 29)	1 recipe
2 tbl	pine nuts	2 tbl

1. Preheat oven to 475°F (240°C). Shape pizza dough according to instructions in Step 3 on page 16.

2. Arrange cheese over dough. Spoon pesto over cheese. Garnish with pine nuts and bake until browned and bubbly (about 18 minutes). Serve hot.

Makes one 16-inch (40-cm) pizza.

The Makings of a Great Pizza

The best pizzas all have one thing in common: they are made from the best-quality ingredients.

- *Use a good grade of olive oil for pizza dough and cooked sauces. Save the finest grades (virgin or extra-virgin) for drizzling over pizza just before baking.*

- *Use the best-quality cheese, preferably imported. Buy a block of aged Parmesan cheese (not pregrated) and grate it just before using. Use fresh whole mozzarella cheese packed in its own whey, if available; otherwise use a premium brand of packaged whole mozzarella (not presliced or pregrated).*

- *Use fresh herbs when possible; If you use dried herbs, purchase them in small quantities from a market with a rapid turnover.*

- *Use fresh garlic, prepared shortly before using. Garlic salt or powder does not provide the same flavor as fresh garlic.*

STOCKING A PIZZA PANTRY

The makings for a great pizza are probably already in your cupboard, refrigerator, or freezer. In addition to the ingredients below, try using carefully selected leftovers for a quick meal.

Staples

Olive oil
Packaged dry yeast
Polenta
Salt
Semolina
Unbleached flour
Whole wheat flour

Prepared Doughs and Crusts

French bread
Frozen bread dough
Frozen pizza crusts
Packaged ready-to-use pizza
    crusts
Pita bread

Herbs and Spices

Basil
Garlic
Oregano
Parsley
Peppercorns
Rosemary

Vegetables

Artichoke hearts or whole baby
    artichokes, marinated
Green chiles, canned
Mushrooms, dried or canned
Olives (black, green, or Greek
    Kalamata)
Pickled hot peppers
    (pepperoncini)
Roasted red peppers, canned
Sun-dried tomatoes, dry-
    packed or bottled in oil
Tomato paste, canned or in
    tubes
Tomatoes, imported canned

Meats, Cheese, and Seafood

Anchovies, canned or in tubes
Cheese (see page 74)
Dried sausages
Ham, canned
Smoked salmon
Smoked turkey

Pizza alle Funghi

The common button mushroom (agaricus bospirum) works well for this artichoke-and-mushroom topped pizza. For a special treat, try cultivated or wild oyster mushrooms or porcini (also called cèpes), perhaps the most popular wild variety. Use marinated "baby" artichokes or artichoke hearts for this recipe. Cut them in halves or, if they are large, in quarters for easier eating.

1 recipe	pizza dough (see pages 15–21)	1 recipe
6	marinated "baby" artichokes or artichoke hearts	6
½ lb	mushrooms, thinly sliced	225 g
¾ cup	grated Parmesan cheese	175 ml
⅓ cup	grated mozzarella cheese	85 ml
½ cup	finely minced green onion	125 ml
as needed	freshly ground black pepper	as needed
as needed	olive oil	as needed

1. Preheat oven to 450°F (230°C).

2. Shape pizza dough according to instructions in Step 3 on page 16.

3. Arrange artichokes on the surface of the dough. Follow with mushrooms, Parmesan, mozzarella, green onion, and pepper. Drizzle with olive oil. Bake until well-browned and puffy (about 20–25 minutes). Serve hot.

Makes one 16-inch (40-cm) pizza.

Pizza Parma

This pie is ablaze with Italian color: the red of the peppers, the white of the cheese, and a spangle of fresh green parsley (see photo on page 43). Present it on a rustic wooden cutting board with a shaker of hot-pepper flakes.

1 recipe	pizza dough (see pages 15–21)	1 recipe
¼ lb	prosciutto, thinly sliced	115 g
2	red bell peppers, roasted and sliced (see opposite page)	2
½ cup	grated mozzarella cheese	125 ml
½ cup	grated Parmesan cheese	125 ml
¼ cup	minced Italian parsley	60 ml
as needed	olive oil	as needed

1. Preheat oven to 450°F (230°C).

2. Shape pizza dough according to instructions in Step 3 on page 16.

3. Arrange slices of prosciutto on the surface of the dough. Add peppers and cover with mozzarella and Parmesan cheeses, and parsley. Drizzle olive oil over surface.

4. Bake until well-browned and puffy (about 20–25 minutes). Serve hot.

Makes one 16-inch (40-cm) pizza.

ROASTING RED PEPPERS

Throughout Italy, Spain, and southern France, cooks roast sweet red peppers and serve them as a salad or add them to a variety of dishes. A few strips of roasted red peppers add vibrant color and flavor to pizza. Although bottled roasted red peppers are widely available, preparing them yourself is simple and far more economical.

2. Peel peppers; halve; remove stem and seeds. Lay halves flat and use dull side of a small knife to scrape away any black bits of skin and stray seeds. Slice into ¼-inch (.6-cm) strips.

1. Hold peppers over an open gas flame or charcoal fire, or place them under a broiler. Turn often until blackened on all sides. Transfer peppers to a paper bag; close and set aside until cool (15–20 minutes).

Pizza alle Pesto e Fontina

It's worth tucking away a jar or two of frozen pesto during the summer when fresh basil is in abundance so that later in the year you can make this irresistible meatless pizza. For the best flavor, use imported fontina (see page 72).

3 tbl	olive oil	3 tbl
½ lb	mushrooms, thinly sliced	225 g
1 recipe	pizza dough (see pages 15–21)	1 recipe
2 cups	grated fontina cheese	500 ml
1 recipe	Pesto Pizza Sauce (see page 29)	1 recipe

1. Preheat oven to 450°F (230°C). Heat 2 tablespoons of the oil in a large frying pan over medium-high heat. Add mushrooms and cook, stirring often, until mushrooms are lightly browned and liquid has cooked away. Remove pan from heat.

2. Shape pizza dough according to instructions in Step 3 on page 16. Brush dough evenly with some of the oil in which mushrooms were cooked.

3. Sprinkle cheese evenly over the dough. Arrange mushrooms over cheese; drizzle with remaining oil.

4. Bake on lowest rack of oven until crust is well-browned (about 25 minutes). Spoon pesto evenly over pizza. Return to oven just long enough to heat pesto (1–2 minutes). Serve hot.

Makes one 16-inch (40-cm) pizza.

GORGONZOLA-PROSCIUTTO PIZZA

This recipe teams blue-veined Gorgonzola and traditional whole-milk mozzarella cheese (see page 72) with prosciutto—the salty, air-dried ham native to Parma.

3 cloves	garlic, unpeeled	3 cloves
2 cups	boiling water	500 ml
1 recipe	pizza dough (see pages 15–21)	1 recipe
1 recipe	Basic Tomato Pizza Sauce (see page 25)	1 recipe
2½ cups	grated mozzarella cheese	600 ml
½ cup	crumbled Gorgonzola cheese	125 ml
¼ lb	sliced prosciutto, cut into strips	115 g

1. Preheat oven to 450°F (230°C). Add garlic to the boiling water in a small saucepan; boil for 1 minute. Drain, peel, then slice garlic thinly.

2. Shape pizza dough according to instructions in Step 3 on page 16.

3. Spread sauce over the dough. Sprinkle with garlic, then with mozzarella and Gorgonzola cheeses. Arrange prosciutto strips over cheeses.

4. Bake on lowest rack of oven until crust is well-browned (15–20 minutes). Serve hot.

Makes one 16-inch (40-cm) pizza.

ABOUT ANCHOVIES

The pungent, salted-fish flavor of anchovies is something pizza lovers typically either relish or detest; few are ambivalent about this oily-fleshed salt-water fish. Anchovies are widely available in supermarkets as whole oil-packed fillets or in paste form, packed in tubes. Far superior in flavor are salt-packed anchovies, which are worth looking for at specialty food stores and Italian markets.

PIZZA PALERMO

This simple pizza from Palermo, along the northern coast of Sicily, is a fine way to show off your home-grown plum tomatoes or the best vine-ripened Italian-style tomatoes you can find at the market. A fruity virgin olive oil and the best-quality mozzarella (see page 74) are other musts.

1	tomato, peeled, seeded, and chopped (see page 28)	1
3 tbl	minced fresh basil	3 tbl
as needed	virgin olive oil	as needed
2 tbl	minced green onion	2 tbl
3 tbl	minced garlic (see pages 30)	3 tbl
1 recipe	pizza dough (see pages 15–21)	1 recipe
½ cup	paper-thin slices red onion	125 ml
1½ cups	grated mozzarella cheese	350 ml
1½ cups	freshly grated Parmesan cheese	350 ml
2	anchovy fillets, sliced lengthwise	2

1. Combine tomato, basil, 2 tablespoons of the olive oil, and green onion; set aside to marinate for at least 30 minutes or up to 8 hours. Combine garlic and 1 tablespoon olive oil in a small bowl and set aside for 30 minutes.

2. Preheat oven to 425°F (220°C). Shape pizza dough according to instructions in Step 3 on page 16.

3. Combine garlic and tomato mixtures and spread over dough. Top with onion slices and mozzarella and Parmesan cheeses. Arrange anchovies on top. Drizzle surface with a little additional olive oil. Bake until the edges are browned and the top is bubbly (about 12–15 minutes). Serve immediately.

Makes one 16-inch (40-cm) pizza.

Pizza alle Pancetta

*Sweet red onions give this pizza a rosy hue (see photo on page 19),
while pancetta, a type of peppery unsmoked bacon available at
delicatessens and Italian markets, provides authentic flavor. If you
can't find pancetta, you can substitute bacon.*

3 tbl	olive oil	3 tbl
1	red onion, thinly slivered	1
1 recipe	pizza dough (see pages 15–21)	1 recipe
¼ lb	pancetta, cut into ½-inch-wide (1.25-cm) strips	115 g
1 recipe	Basic Tomato Pizza Sauce (see page 25)	1 recipe
2 cups	grated mozzarella cheese	500 ml
¼ cup	grated Romano or Parmesan cheese	60 ml

1. Preheat oven to 450°F (230°C). Heat oil in a large frying pan
   over moderate heat. Add onion and cook, stirring often, until
   soft but not browned (8–10 minutes). Remove onion with a
   slotted spoon and reserve.

2. Shape pizza dough according to instructions in Step 3 on
   page 16.

3. Add pancetta to same pan and cook, stirring often, until it
   begins to brown (about 3 minutes). Drain on paper towels,
   reserving oil in pan.

4. Brush dough evenly with oil remaining in frying pan. Spread
   sauce over the pizza. Sprinkle evenly with cheeses. Arrange
   onion and pancetta evenly over surface.

7. Bake on lowest rack of oven until crust is well-browned
   (15–20 minutes). Serve hot.

Makes one 16-inch (40-cm) pizza.

PIZZA DEL NORD

An excellent melting cheese with a buttery, nutty flavor, fontina transforms a plain cheese pizza into something memorable.

1 recipe	pizza dough (see pages 15–21)	1 recipe
as needed	olive oil	as needed
1½ cups	peeled, seeded, and chopped tomatoes (see page 28)	350 ml
1½ cups	grated fontina cheese	350 ml
3 tbl	paper-thin garlic slices (see page 30)	3 tbl
¼ cup	diced provolone	60 ml
¼ cup	coarsely chopped Italian parsley	60 ml
1 cup	grated Parmesan cheese	250 ml
as needed	minced Italian parsley, for garnish (optional)	as needed

1. Preheat oven to 425°F (220°C). Shape pizza dough according to instructions in Step 3 on page 16.

2. Brush dough with olive oil. Spread tomatoes over the dough and top with fontina, garlic, provolone, and parsley. Sprinkle Parmesan cheese over top of pizza. Drizzle with additional olive oil.

3. Bake until the edges are browned and the top is bubbly (about 12–15 minutes). Garnish with additional parsley, if desired. Serve hot.

Makes one 16-inch (40-cm) pizza.

ABOUT PARSLEY

An important component to almost all the world's cuisines, fresh parsley imparts a clean, fresh, flavor and pleasing color to hundreds of dishes. The flat-leaf variety known as Italian parsley has a more pungent flavor than the curly-leaf type widely used as a garnish. Given the ready availability and affordability of fresh parsley, there is little reason to use the dried form.

Pizza Côte d'Azur

Along the coast of southern France, pizza is as popular as it is in Italy. This pizza is flavored with herbes de Provence, a commercial blend of dried thyme, lavender, summer savory, basil, and rosemary—herbs typical of the south of France. Look for oil-packed niçoise olives, another specialty of southern France, and Gruyère cheese (see page 72) at supermarkets and in specialty food stores.

¼ cup	olive oil	60 ml
2	onions, thinly slivered	2
2 cloves	garlic, minced	2 cloves
½ tsp	dried herbes de Provence	½ tsp
2 tbl	chopped Italian parsley	2 tbl
1 recipe	pizza dough (see pages 15–21)	1 recipe
1 recipe	Basic Tomato Pizza Sauce (see page 25)	1 recipe
1½ cups	grated Gruyère cheese	350 ml
1 can (2 oz)	anchovy fillets, well drained	1 can (60 g)
¼ cup	small niçoise olives	60 ml

1. Preheat oven to 450°F (230°C). Heat oil in a large frying pan over moderate heat. Add onions and cook, stirring often, until soft but not browned (10–12 minutes); remove from heat.

2. Spoon about 1 tablespoon of the hot oil from the pan into a small bowl; mix in garlic, herbes de Provence, and parsley.

3. Shape pizza dough according to instructions in Step 3 on page 16.

4. Spread sauce over the pizza and sprinkle evenly with cheese. Spread onions over cheese. Arrange anchovies and olives over onions. Sprinkle evenly with garlic-and-herb mixture.

5. Bake until crust is well-browned (20–25 minutes). Serve hot.

Makes one 16-inch (40-cm) pizza.

Pizza Siciliano

Sicilians know you don't need tomatoes to make a pizza, especially when the new spring garlic crop is in. Because the toppings for this pizza are so simple, it requires the best ingredients: young garlic, virgin olive oil, fresh oregano, and top-quality Parmesan cheese (see page 74). Serve this pizza on its own or as an accompaniment to roast chicken or grilled fish.

1 recipe	pizza dough (see pages 15–21)	1 recipe
1 recipe	Garlic-Oregano Pizza Sauce (see page 31)	1 recipe
as needed	olive oil	as needed
2	red bell peppers, roasted and sliced (see page 45)	2
as needed	grated Parmesan cheese	as needed

1. Preheat oven to 450°F (230°C). Shape pizza dough according to instructions in Step 3 on page 16.

2. Spread the sauce on the pizza dough. Drizzle with olive oil, and top with red peppers.

3. Bake until well-browned and puffy (about 20 minutes). Dust with Parmesan cheese. Serve hot.

Makes one 16-inch (40-cm) pizza.

A Pizza By Any Other Name

Few traditional foods come in as many varieties as pizza. In Italy and elsewhere, pizza may assume many different forms and go by other names. Popular Italian flatbreads such as focaccia and pizzette (see pages 58–63), as well as the turnover known as calzone (see pages 66–69) are no doubt the ancestors of modern pizza. Italy's neighbors have developed their own forms of pizza: Sicily is the birthplace of a pizza-like soufflé (see pages 55–56), while France is the home of flammekueche (see pages 56–57), pissaladière (see pages 64–65), and a sweet pastry "pizza" (see pages 90–91).

SICILIAN PIZZA SOUFFLÉ

In Sicily, this rich, puffy creation is called a "pizza soufflé." The topping actually does puff up and brown slightly, resulting in a most unusual tomato-less pizza. No addition could possibly improve it. For the best flavor, use good Italian Gorgonzola and whole-milk ricotta cheeses.

1 recipe	pizza dough (see pages 15–21)	1 recipe
1½ cups	ricotta cheese	350 ml
1 cup	Gorgonzola cheese, crumbled	250 ml
3	eggs	3
½ cup+2 tbl	minced Italian parsley	125 ml+2 tbl
2 cloves	garlic, minced	2 cloves
1 cup	grated Parmesan cheese	250 ml
as needed	olive oil	as needed

1. Preheat oven to 450°F (230°C). Shape pizza dough according to instructions in Step 3 on page 16.

2. In a large mixing bowl, combine ricotta and Gorgonzola cheeses, eggs, ½ cup (125 ml) of the parsley, garlic, and half of the Parmesan cheese. Spread this mixture over the surface of the dough. Drizzle with olive oil and dust with remaining Parmesan cheese.

3. Bake until well-browned and puffy (about 20–25 minutes). Serve hot, garnished with remaining parsley.

Makes one 16-inch (40-cm) pizza.

PIZZA D'ALSACE

The flammekueche ("flaming tart") is the Alsatian version of pizza. Note that the Fromage Blanc needs to chill for 12 hours.

Fromage Blanc

¾ cup	ricotta cheese	175 ml
3 tbl	plain yogurt	3 tbl
pinch	salt	pinch
2 recipes	Neapolitan Pizza Dough (see page 18)	2 recipes
¼ lb	slab bacon, cubed	115 g
1 tbl	olive oil	1 tbl
1½ cups	thinly sliced yellow onion	350 ml
1	egg	1
1 tbl	flour	1 tbl
¼ cup	grated Gruyère cheese	60 ml
2 tbl	water	2 tbl

1. To prepare Fromage Blanc, combine all ingredients in a blender and blend 30 seconds. Chill 12 hours before using.

2. Shape pizza dough according to instructions in Step 3 on page 16, rolling out dough to a round as large as your oven can accommodate. You can form 2 smaller rounds, if you prefer.

3. In a medium skillet over moderate heat, cook bacon in olive oil until well-browned. Transfer bacon to a plate with a slotted spoon and add onion to drippings in skillet. Sauté until slightly softened (about 5 minutes). Cool to room temperature.

4. Preheat oven to 425°F (220°C). Whisk together Fromage Blanc, egg, and the 1 tablespoon flour.

5. Spread dough with Fromage Blanc mixture to within ¾ inch (1.9 cm) of edge. Top with onions and bacon and sprinkle with grated cheese. Brush edge of dough with the 2 tablespoons water. Bake until golden brown (15–20 minutes). Serve hot.

Makes one large tart.

FOCACCIA BASILICO

The grandfather of Neopolitan pizza is focaccia.

1¼ cups	warm water (105°F or 41°C)	300 ml
¾ tsp	sugar	¾ tsp
1 pkg (1 tbl)	active dry yeast	1 pkg (1 tbl)
2¾ cups	unbleached flour	650 ml
as needed	olive oil	as needed
½ cup	minced onion	125 ml
⅓ cup	minced fresh basil	85 ml
1½ tsp	coarse salt	1½ tsp
½ tsp	freshly ground black pepper	½ tsp
as needed	cornmeal, for dusting	as needed

1. Combine ½ cup (125 ml) of the water, the sugar, and yeast in a large bowl. Set aside 10 minutes. Stir in ¾ cup (175 ml) of the flour, cover, and let rise 2½ hours.

2. While dough is rising, heat 3 tablespoons oil in a skillet over low heat. Add onion and sauté until onion is soft but not browned (about 15 minutes). Remove from heat and stir in basil, ½ teaspoon of the salt, and pepper.

3. Add the remaining flour to dough and beat well. Combine 2 tablespoons olive oil and the remaining warm water, then add to dough. Beat until dough forms a mass. Turn out onto a lightly floured surface and knead until dough is shiny and smooth, 8–10 minutes. Transfer dough to a lightly oiled bowl and turn to coat all sides with oil. Cover and let rise until doubled in bulk, about 1½ hours.

4. Preheat oven to 450°F (230°C). Punch dough down and roll into a large rectangle about ½-inch (1.25-cm) thick. Transfer to a baker's peel or baking sheet sprinkled with cornmeal. Spread top with onion mixture. Drizzle with additional olive oil. Sprinkle with the remaining coarse salt and bake until golden, about 15 minutes. Cool slightly on a rack; serve warm.

Makes 1 large flatbread.

FOCACCIA BIANCA

Slathered with herb-tinged onions sautéed in olive oil, this savory pizza-like flatbread is delicious as an appetizer, an accompaniment to grilled meats, or a flavorful sandwich bread.

Onion Topping

2 tbl	butter	2 tbl
2 tbl	olive oil	2 tbl
2	onions, thinly sliced and separated into rings	2
½ tsp	dried sage	½ tsp
⅓ cup	grated Parmesan cheese	85 ml
1 recipe	Deep-Dish Pizza Dough (see page 22)	1 recipe

1. Preheat oven to 425°F (220°C). To prepare Onion Topping, in a large frying pan over medium-low heat, heat butter with oil. Add onions; cook, stirring occasionally, until soft but not browned (15–20 minutes). Stir in sage. Remove from heat and stir in Parmesan cheese.

2. Shape pizza dough according to instructions in Step 3 on page 16, rolling out dough about ½-inch (1.25-cm) thick into a large rectangle or round.

3. Spoon the topping over the dough. Bake until golden brown (15–20 minutes). Serve hot.

Makes 1 large flatbread.

Gorgonzola Pizzette

Dimpled with pools of melted Gorgonzola and Parmesan cheeses, these miniature rounds are a variation on classic Italian flatbread (see photo on page 61).

1 recipe	Deep-Dish Pizza Dough	1 recipe
as needed	oil, for pan	as needed
as needed	olive oil	as needed
½ cup	crumbled Gorgonzola cheese	125 ml
⅓ cup	freshly grated Parmesan cheese	⅓ cup

1. Preheat oven to 425°F (220°C). Divide dough into six equal portions. Roll and stretch each portion to a circle about 6 inches in diameter. Place on two large, oiled baking pans.

2. Make depressions in dough, using your thumb or the end of a wooden spoon, at 1-inch intervals. Brush rounds lightly with olive oil. Sprinkle evenly with Gorgonzola and Parmesan cheeses. Let stand until dough looks puffy (10–12 minutes).

3. Bake until golden brown (12–15 minutes). Serve hot or cold.

Makes 6 small flatbreads.

About Balsamic Vinegar

This aromatic sweet/tart vinegar is aged for several years or even for decades in wooden barrels before being bottled. Its distinctive mellow character is greatly appreciated by Italian cooks, who use it to enrich stews, dress salads, enliven fresh fruit, and even perk up pizza toppings.

Pizzette dell'Estate

This pizza-like flatbread makes a perfect snack, picnic, or lunch dish.

1 recipe	pizza dough (see pages 15–21)	1 recipe
as needed	cornmeal, for dusting	as needed
1 tbl	unsalted butter	1 tbl
6 tbl	olive oil	6 tbl
1 tbl	minced garlic	1 tbl
¾ cup	minced onion	175 ml
½ cup	chopped mushrooms	125 ml
2 tbl	balsamic vinegar (see below)	2 tbl
¼ cup	chopped fresh basil	60 ml
1 cup	peeled, seeded, and chopped tomatoes (see page 28)	250 ml
4 tbl	grated Parmesan cheese	4 tbl
4	anchovy fillets, cut into 4 strips each	4

1. Preheat oven to 450°F (230°C). Divide dough into 4 equal portions. Roll each quarter into a small round, about 4–5 inches (10–12.5 cm) in diameter. Dust a large, heavy baking sheet with cornmeal and transfer rounds to baking sheet.

2. In a medium skillet over low heat, heat butter and 2 tablespoons of the oil. Add garlic and onion and sauté for 5 minutes, until they are fragrant and slightly softened (about 10 minutes). Add mushrooms and cook 5 minutes more.

3. Turn heat to high and, when mixture begins to sizzle, add vinegar. Whisk 10 seconds and remove from heat. Stir in basil.

4. Divide onion mixture among the rounds, spreading it evenly over the surface. Garnish each round with a quarter of the tomatoes and dust each with 1 tablespoon Parmesan cheese. Arrange anchovy strips over each round. Drizzle each with one tablespoon of the remaining olive oil. Bake until browned (about 12–16 minutes). Cool on racks. Serve hot or cold.

Makes 4 small flatbreads.

PISSALADIÈRE

All over the French Riviera, you find "the pizza of Nice": pissaladière.

as needed	olive oil	as needed
¼ cup	unsalted butter	60 ml
4	yellow onions, thinly sliced	4
3 cloves	garlic, minced	3 cloves
1 tsp	minced fresh thyme or ½ teaspoon dried	1 tsp
to taste	salt and black pepper	to taste
1 can (2 oz)	anchovy fillets in oil	1 can (60 g)
12–15	Kalamata olives, pitted	12–15
1 recipe	pizza dough (see pages 15–21)	1 recipe
as needed	cornmeal, for dusting	as needed
¼ cup	minced Italian parsley	60 ml
¼ cup	chopped fresh basil	60 ml

1. Preheat oven to 400°F (205°C). In a large, heavy skillet over medium heat, heat 3 tablespoons olive oil and butter. Add onions and cook gently for 5 minutes. Add garlic, thyme, salt, and pepper. Cook 20 minutes, or until onions are very soft but not brown. Taste; adjust seasoning if necessary.

2. Put 2 anchovy fillets and half the olives in a blender. Add a few drops olive oil and blend. Add more oil as necessary to make a smooth paste.

3. To assemble pissaladière, roll dough out into a square or circle. Transfer to a baking sheet dusted with cornmeal. Spread with anchovy and olive paste and cover with onion slices. Arrange remaining anchovies over onions in a crisscross pattern. Slice remaining olives; arrange between anchovies. Drizzle with a little olive oil and dust with 2 tablespoons each parsley and basil. Bake until well browned (about 30–35 minutes). Cool slightly, then sprinkle with remaining herbs just before serving. Cut while still warm.

Makes one 16-inch (40-cm) pizza.

Calzone con Spinaci

A calzone is a savory Italian turnover. Shaped like bulging half moons, the smaller ones are eaten out of hand, as a snack or a quick lunch; large ones require a knife and fork. Cutting into a hot calzone and releasing the molten filling is part of the pleasure of this fragrant dish, but small ones should be cooled slightly to firm the filling and avoid burning the fingers.

1½ cups	lightly cooked fresh spinach, squeezed dry	350 ml
1¼ cups	ricotta cheese	300 ml
3 tbl	freshly grated Parmesan cheese	3 tbl
¼ cup	pitted and chopped Kalamata olives	60 ml
¼ cup	minced Italian parsley	60 ml
1 recipe	pizza dough (see pages 15–21)	1 recipe
½ cup	grated mozzarella cheese	125 ml
½ cup	shredded prosciutto (optional)	125 ml
1	egg mixed with 1 tablespoon water	1
as needed	olive oil	as needed
as needed	cornmeal, for dusting	as needed

1. Preheat oven to 475°F (240°C). In a bowl combine spinach, ricotta, Parmesan cheese, olives, and parsley. Set aside.

2. Roll dough out on a lightly floured surface into 1 large or 2 small rounds, ¼ inch (.6 cm) thick. Spread spinach mixture over bottom half of the dough, leaving a ½-inch (1.25-cm) border. Cover spinach with mozzarella and prosciutto, if used.

3. Brush border with egg mixture, then fold top half over the filling, moistening and pinching edges together or pressing with tines of a fork to seal. Brush top with olive oil. Sprinkle a large baking sheet with cornmeal. Place calzone on prepared baking sheet. Let rise until puffy (10–15 minutes).

4. Bake on center rack until golden (about 12–15 minutes). Remove from oven and brush again with olive oil. If calzone will be eaten out of hand, let cool slightly before serving.

Makes 2 small or 1 large calzone.

Calzone con Pomodori

This style of pizza turnover is said to have originated in Naples, and the tomato and mozzarella filling is distinctively Neapolitan.

as needed	olive oil	as needed
1	onion, finely chopped	1
1 clove	garlic, minced	1 clove
1 cup	ricotta cheese	1 cup
¼ cup	chopped sun-dried tomatoes	60 ml
2 tbl	chopped Italian parsley	2 tbl
1 recipe	Deep-Dish Pizza Dough (see page 22)	1 recipe
2 cups	sliced prosciutto or dry salami, cut into strips	500 ml
2 cups	grated mozzarella cheese	500 ml
as needed	cornmeal, for dusting	as needed

1. Preheat oven to 450°F (230°C). In a medium skillet heat 1 tablespoon oil over moderate heat; add onion and cook, stirring often, until soft but not browned. Mix in garlic, then remove from heat. In a medium bowl mix ricotta cheese with dried tomatoes and parsley; stir in cooked onion mixture.

2. Roll dough out on a lightly floured surface into 1 large or 2 small rounds, ¼-inch (.6-cm) thick. Spread the ricotta filling over bottom half of dough, leaving a ½-inch (1.25-cm) border.

3. Sprinkle prosciutto strips and mozzarella cheese over ricotta filling. Fold dough in half over filling, moistening with a few drops of water and pinching edges together or pressing with tines of a fork to seal.

4. Sprinkle a large baking sheet with cornmeal. Place calzone on prepared baking sheet. Let rise until puffy (10–15 minutes). Brush top with olive oil. Bake on center rack until golden (about 12–15 minutes). Remove from oven and brush again with olive oil. Serve hot.

Makes 1 large or 2 medium calzone.

CONTEMPORARY CLASSICS

The definition of a pizza is changing. Heavy crusts soggy with boring canned sauces and laden with rubbery toppings are giving way to delightfully new pizza creations. This section features contemporary specialties that emphasize what's fresh and readily available. The result is an amazing variety of innovative pizzas that are as flavorful as they are enjoyable to make and eat.

Pizza di Mare

A new twist on an old favorite, this pizza is a pièce de résistance for lovers of seafood. The Rouille Sauce combines fresh herbs and other seasonings with a classic mayonnaise base.

4 oz	shelled and deveined shrimp, cut in half lengthwise	115 g
4 oz	scallops, cut in quarters	115 g
1½ tbl	olive oil	1½ tbl
2 tsp	lemon juice	2 tsp
1 tsp	minced peeled garlic (see page 30)	1 tsp
to taste	salt and freshly ground black pepper	to taste
⅓ cup	peeled, thinly sliced red onion	85 ml
½ cup	thinly sliced zucchini	125 ml
1 recipe	pizza dough (see pages 15–21)	1 recipe
1 cup	grated Gruyère or provolone cheese	250 ml
⅓ cup	peeled, seeded, and chopped tomato (see page 28)	85 ml
3 tbl	grated Parmesan cheese	3 tbl
1 tbl	chopped Italian parsley	1 tbl

Rouille Sauce

1 tbl	dry white wine	1 tbl
pinch	ground saffron	pinch
as needed	olive oil	as needed
⅛–¼ tsp	crushed hot-pepper flakes	⅛–¼ tsp
1	egg yolk	1
1 tsp	fresh lemon juice	1 tsp
½ tsp	minced, peeled garlic	½ tsp
⅛ tsp	salt	⅛ tsp
1 tbl	chopped fresh basil	1 tbl

1. In a small bowl toss shrimp, scallops, 1 tablespoon of the olive oil, lemon juice, ½ teaspoon of the garlic, and a sprinkling of salt and pepper. Marinate 30–45 minutes. Drain and discard marinade. Set shellfish mixture aside. Preheat oven to 425°F (220°C).

2. To prepare Rouille Sauce, mix wine and saffron and steep for 10 minutes. Heat 2 teaspoons oil in a small skillet. Add pepper flakes and cook 10 seconds. Remove skillet from heat and add wine-saffron mixture. (Stand back—it will sizzle.) Let cool. In a small mixing bowl, whisk egg yolk with lemon juice, garlic, and salt. Gradually begin adding ¼ cup olive oil, drop by drop, whisking continuously. As sauce begins to thicken, add oil a little faster. When all oil is added, stir in pepper mixture and basil. Set sauce aside.

3. Heat ½ tablespoon olive oil in a skillet. Add remaining garlic and onion. Cook about 20 seconds over high heat, stirring constantly. Add the zucchini and cook, stirring constantly, another 10 seconds. Remove from heat and set aside.

4. Shape pizza dough according to instructions in Step 3 on page 16. Brush dough with olive oil. Sprinkle ½ cup of the Gruyère cheese over the top of the dough, leaving a 1-inch (2.5 cm) border. Spread the cooked onion, garlic, and zucchini over the cheese; top with tomato. Sprinkle remaining ½ cup (125 ml) Gruyère cheese over the top. Sprinkle with salt and pepper.

5. Bake until crust is well-browned (15–20 minutes). Remove the pizza from the oven and preheat broiler. Scatter the seafood over the pizza. Place under broiler until seafood is almost done (1–2 minutes). Again remove pizza from oven and spoon Rouille Sauce over top. Sprinkle with Parmesan cheese and pepper. Return pizza to broiler until the sauce is bubbly (about 2 minutes). Remove from the oven and sprinkle with parsley. Let rest 5 minutes before serving.

Makes one 16-inch (40-cm) pizza.

South Side Stuffed Pizza

This torte-like pizza has a meatless filling.

as needed	olive oil	as needed
1	onion, thinly slivered	1
½ lb	mushrooms, thinly sliced	225 g
1 cup	sliced red or green bell pepper	250 ml
2 cloves	garlic, minced	2 cloves
½ tsp each	salt and dried oregano	½ tsp each
⅛ tsp each	black pepper and dried marjoram	⅛ tsp each
1 recipe	Deep-Dish Pizza Dough (see page 22)	1 recipe
4 cups	grated Monterey jack cheese	900 ml
1 recipe	Basic Tomato Pizza Sauce (see page 25)	1 recipe
⅔ cup	freshly grated Parmesan cheese	150 ml

1. Preheat oven to 450°F (230°C). In a large frying pan over medium-high heat, heat ¼ cup (60 ml) olive oil. Add onion, mushrooms, and bell pepper, stirring often, until onion is soft. Mix in garlic, salt, oregano, pepper, and marjoram, then remove from heat and set aside.

2. Oil a 15-inch (37.5-cm) deep-dish pizza pan. Divide dough into two portions, one about a third larger than the other. Roll out larger portion to about a 16-inch (40-cm) round. Place dough in pan, pressing it up the sides of pan to reach top edge.

3. Sprinkle dough evenly with 3 cups (700 ml) of the jack cheese. Spread vegetable mixture over cheese.

4. Roll out remaining dough to a 15-inch (37.5-cm) round; place over vegetables, folding rim of dough lining pan over top layer of dough. Spread tomato sauce over top layer of dough. Sprinkle evenly with remaining jack cheese. Top with Parmesan cheese. Bake on lowest rack of oven until crust and cheese are well-browned (25–30 minutes). Let stand for 2–3 minutes before cutting into wedges to serve.

Makes one 15-inch (37.5-cm) stuffed pizza.

A Treasury of Cheeses for Pizza

For many people, the most important part of a pizza is the cheese topping. Here are some of the most popular cheeses for pizza:

Feta Of Greek origin, feta is salty and crumbly, traditionally made from sheep's or goat's milk. Its unique consistency, flavor, and lower fat content make it increasingly popular as a pizza topping.

Fontina This cow's milk cheese has a creamy, smooth texture, nutty flavor, and earthy aroma that make it excellent for pizza.

Gorgonzola Made from cow's milk, Gorgonzola is one of Italy's most famous blue-veined cheeses. Used crumbled, Gorgonzola makes a rich, pungent topping for pizza.

Gruyère A Swiss import, Gruyère is mild-tasting, with a semi-firm texture that is ideal for grating over pizza. The French equivalent to Gruyère is Comté.

Mozzarella Originally made from water-buffalo milk, most mozzarella is now produced from cow's milk. Many consider it the ideal cheese for pizza, especially when it is imported and very fresh, packed in its own whey. Packaged domestic varieties bear little resemblance to fresh mozzarella.

Parmesan (Parmigiano Reggiano) A cow's milk cheese that is one of Italy's most famous exports, this cheese is nutty, golden, and sharp. It gets drier with age and is the classic grating cheese for pizza. Ideally it should be purchased in chunk form and grated just before using.

Pecorino Romano The best-known pecorino (sheep's milk) cheese, this variety is pale and moist when young, becoming more tangy and harder as it ages. It makes a highly flavorful pizza topping.

Provolone A cow's milk cheese, provolone is mild, firm, and melts well. Its subtle flavor blends perfectly with a wide variety of other pizza toppings.

CHICAGO-STYLE VEGETARIAN PIZZA

The Windy City is famous for its deep-dish pizzas, including this vegetarian version.

1 head	garlic	1 head
as needed	olive oil	as needed
1 recipe	Deep-Dish Pizza Dough (see page 22)	1 recipe
1 bunch	spinach, washed and drained	1 bunch
1	green bell pepper, seeded and cut into strips	1
1 recipe	Basic Tomato Pizza Sauce (see page 25)	1 recipe
1½ cups	grated mozzarella cheese	350 ml
½ cup	grated dry Monterey jack cheese	125 ml

1. Preheat oven to 350°F (175°C). Slice about ½ inch (1.25 cm) from top of garlic head. Remove some of the papery covering from garlic but leave the head intact. Place the garlic in a small baking dish and pour 2 tablespoons oil over it. Bake until garlic is tender (50–60 minutes). Cool slightly and set aside.

2. Increase oven temperature to 450°F (230°C). Oil a 15-inch (37.5-cm) deep-dish pizza pan and line with dough as in Step 2 on page 73. Bake for 5 minutes and remove from oven.

3. Chop spinach coarsely and cook in a skillet over medium-high heat until wilted. Remove spinach and reserve.

4. Squeeze garlic from papery shell over pizza dough. Arrange spinach, bell pepper strips, sauce, and cheeses over dough. Bake until cheeses are melted and crust is lightly browned (20 minutes). Serve at once.

Makes one 15-inch (37.5-cm) deep-dish pizza.

CHICAGO-STYLE SAUSAGE PIZZA

This traditional version of Windy-City pizza unites Italian sausage, cheese, mushrooms, and a fresh tomato sauce in a traditional combination; you can substitute sliced pepperoni for the sausage, if you prefer.

¾ lb	bulk Italian sausage	350 g
as needed	olive oil	as needed
1 recipe	Deep-Dish Pizza Dough (see page 22)	1 recipe
4 cups	grated mozzarella cheese	900 ml
½ lb	mushrooms, thinly sliced	225 g
1 recipe	Spicy Pizza Sauce (see page 26)	1 recipe
⅓ cup	grated Parmesan cheese	85 ml

1. Preheat oven to 450°F (230°C). Crumble sausage meat into a large frying pan over medium-high heat. Cook, stirring often, until lightly browned. Pour off drippings and discard. Set sausage aside.

2. Oil a 15-inch (37.5-cm) deep-dish pizza pan and line with dough as in Step 2 on page 73.

3. Sprinkle half of the mozzarella over the dough. Cover with an even layer of mushrooms, then with cooked sausage. Spread the sauce over sausage. Cover with remaining mozzarella and top with the Parmesan cheese.

4. Bake on lowest rack of oven until crust browns well (20–25 minutes). Serve at once.

Makes one 15-inch (37.5-cm) deep-dish pizza.

QUICK PIZZA BAGUETTE

This French-bread pizza makes a good picnic main dish. Add an antipasto assortment, red jug wine or mineral water, and fruit and cookies for dessert. If you wrap the hot, filled loaf tightly in aluminum foil, then insulate it well with layers of newspaper, it will stay warm for several hours.

1 long loaf	French bread, unsliced	1 long loaf
1	onion, coarsely chopped	1
1 clove	garlic, minced	1 clove
2 tbl	olive oil	2 tbl
½ cup	grated Parmesan cheese	125 ml
1 can (8 oz)	tomato sauce	1 can (225 g)
1 can (4 oz)	sliced mushrooms, drained	1 can (115 g)
¾ tsp	salt	¾ tsp
½ tsp	dried oregano	½ tsp
to taste	freshly ground black pepper	to taste
1 lb	lean ground beef or turkey	450 g
1	egg, slightly beaten	1
½ cup	shredded mozzarella cheese	125 ml

1. Preheat oven to 375°F (190°C). Cut a slice about ½ inch (1.25 cm) deep from the top of the loaf of French bread. Set top crust aside. Scoop out most of the bread, leaving the crust intact. Tear bread into small pieces to make 1½ cups (350 ml) and set aside.

2. In a skillet over medium-high heat brown onion and garlic in oil. Mix in reserved bread crumbs, Parmesan cheese, tomato sauce, mushrooms, salt, oregano, and pepper. Add ground beef and egg; mix lightly. Spoon into hollowed-out bread shell. Replace top crust and wrap loaf securely in foil. (At this point, loaf can be refrigerated for several hours or overnight.)

3. Bake about 1 hour and 20 minutes. Fold back foil; remove top crust and arrange mozzarella cheese over top. Replace top crust and return loaf to oven. Bake until cheese is melted and bubbly (about 5 minutes). Serve warm.

Serves 6.

PIZZA ON THE GRILL

Purists insist that the key to making good pizza is a wood-fired oven—something you won't find in most home kitchens. Using your outdoor grill, you can duplicate the texture and flavor of pizza baked the traditional way. The next time you're thinking of grilling, think of pizza.

- *First, choose a dough recipe containing a liberal amount of olive oil to keep the crust soft during grilling (see recipes on pages 15 and 21). Shape the dough into small rounds (no more than 8 inches or 20 cm in diameter) and lightly coat the rounds of dough with oil on both sides.*

- *Use hardwood charcoal (not briquettes) and let the fire burn down to red-hot coals. Use this hand test to gauge the temperature of the coals: If you can comfortably hold your hand over the coals while you count slowly to 4, the coals are just about right. If you can hold your hand longer than 4 seconds, you need fresh coals; if the heat is too great to endure for 4 seconds, you need to let the coals burn down a bit more.*

- *Place 2 or 3 rounds of dough at a time on the grill rack, 4–5 inches above the coals, and cook until toasted on the outside and soft on the inside (about a minute on each side). Crusts can be grilled ahead of time, wrapped in plastic wrap when cool, and then sauced and topped when you're ready to serve the pizzas.*

- *Allow the coals to die down a bit while you prepare the sauce and toppings. Place the prepared pizzas on the grill and heat just long enough to cook the toppings. Do not allow the crust to burn. If you prefer, complete the cooking by putting the pizzas under the broiler or in a toaster oven.*

ROASTED NEW-POTATO PIZZA

A California version of traditional Italian potato pizza, this recipe combines a creamy spinach-basil pesto with slices of roasted red potatoes.

as needed	olive oil	as needed
2 cups	thinly sliced red-skinned new potatoes	500 ml
to taste	salt and freshly ground black pepper	to taste
1 recipe	pizza dough (see pages 15–21)	1 recipe
½ cup	minced spinach leaves	125 ml
½ cup	chopped Italian parsley	125 ml
2 tbl	chopped fresh basil	2 tbl
1 tbl	minced garlic	1 tbl
¼ cup	coarsely chopped walnuts	60 ml
¼ cup	grated Parmesan cheese	60 ml

1. Preheat oven to 450°F (230°C). Lightly oil a baking sheet. Place sliced potatoes in a bowl and sprinkle with salt, pepper, and 1 teaspoon of oil. Toss well to coat evenly. Place on prepared baking sheet and roast until lightly browned (about 10 minutes).

2. Shape pizza dough according to instructions in Step 3 on page 16.

3. Place spinach, parsley, basil, garlic, walnuts, 2 tablespoons olive oil, and cheese into a blender or food processor and purée. Spread purée thickly on pizza dough. Place roasted potatoes on top. Bake until dough is lightly browned (about 15 minutes). Serve hot.

Makes one 16-inch (40-cm) pizza.

PITA PIZZAS

When baked at a high temperature, pita bread becomes crisp, just like pizza crust. Make a single pizza for a quick solo supper, or multiply the recipe to feed a whole crowd. These pint-sized pizzas also are good cold or reheated for brown bag lunches or snacks.

For each pita pizza:

1	pita bread	1
1 tsp	olive oil	1 tsp
¼ cup	peeled, seeded, and chopped tomatoes (see page 28)	60 ml
	or	
¼ cup	Basic Tomato Pizza Sauce (see page 25)	60 ml
¼ tsp	finely chopped garlic	¼ tsp
to taste	fresh or dried herbs	to taste
3–4 tbl	grated Parmesan cheese	3–4 tbl

1. Preheat oven to 500°F (260°C). Place the pita bread on a baking sheet and brush lightly with oil.

2. Top with tomatoes or spread with tomato sauce.

3. Scatter garlic and your choice of fresh or dried herbs over top. Sprinkle with Parmesan cheese.

4. Bake until crust is crisp and browned (10–15 minutes).

Makes 1 pita pizza.

Pizza Party Buffet

What better way to celebrate than with a lighthearted make-your-own pizza party? As with any form of entertaining, careful planning is the key to success:

- *Plan to offer an assortment of beverages, a simple antipasto platter or two, and perhaps a large tossed salad (undressed), with a variety of salad dressings. For an easy dessert, how about a fabulous fake "pizza" (see pages 89, 92, and 94)?*

- *Since nobody likes to wait too long for pizza, plan to streamline the assembly process: Have the oven preheated to 450°F (230°C). Set out trays of small, individual pizza crusts. Packaged ready-to-eat, frozen, or pre-grilled crusts (see page 79) are the easiest for a party. Set out a variety of sauces and toppings (see pages 24–33) on trays near the pizza crusts. Include a small bottle of good-quality olive oil for drizzling over the finished pizzas. Have several prepared baking sheets ready nearby, and don't forget a good supply of napkins and plenty of hand towels.*

- *Invite your guests to top the crusts with whatever sauce and toppings they prefer. As they complete their custom-made creations, place the prepared pizzas on the baking sheets you've set aside. As soon as a sheet is filled with pizzas, pop it into the oven, set the timer, and bake pizzas until done. Remove the baked pizzas and put the next batch into the oven.*

- *As soon as a batch of pizzas is done, encourage guests to identify their pizzas and serve themselves. Of course, sampling someone else's pizza is half the fun. Don't forget to have extra crusts, sauce, and toppings on hand for the inevitable second and third helpings.*

Pizza Picante

For those who enjoy pizza even when it isn't more than vaguely Italian, here is a slightly picante version with a Mexican influence.

3 tbl	olive oil	3 tbl
1	onion, thinly sliced	1
½ tsp	ground cumin	½ tsp
½ lb	chorizo sausage	225 g
1 recipe	pizza dough (see pages 15–21)	1 recipe
1 recipe	Spicy Pizza Sauce (see page 26)	1 recipe
3 cups	grated Montcrey jack cheese	700 ml
1 can (4 oz)	diced green chiles, drained	1 can (115 g)

1. Preheat oven to 450°F (230°C). Heat oil in a large frying pan over moderate heat. Add onion and cook, stirring often, until soft but not browned (8–10 minutes); mix in cumin, then transfer onion mixture to a bowl.

2. Remove casings from sausage and crumble into the same pan in which onions were cooked. Cook, stirring often, until lightly browned. Remove sausage from pan with a slotted spoon and drain on paper towels.

3. Shape pizza dough according to instructions in Step 3 on page 16.

4. Spread sauce over the dough. Sprinkle with cheese and spread onions over cheese. Spoon sausage over onions and top with green chiles.

5. Bake on lowest rack of oven until crust browns well (20–25 minutes). Serve hot.

Makes one 16-inch (40-cm) pizza.

POLENTA PIZZA

A cornmeal crust gives this pizza extra crunch. The dough requires no kneading or raising and is ready to use in only a quarter of an hour.

as needed	olive oil	as needed
2 cups	polenta	500 ml
1 cup	cold water	250 ml
1 cup	boiling water	250 ml
2	eggs	2
1 cup	grated mozzarella cheese	250 ml
¼ cup	chopped green onions	60 ml
¼ cup	chopped red bell pepper	60 ml
1 cup	thinly sliced mushrooms	250 ml
2 cups	Basic Tomato Pizza Sauce (see page 25)	500 ml
1 cup	thickly sliced plum tomatoes	250 ml
¼ cup	chopped Italian parsley	60 ml
1 tbl	minced fresh basil	1 tbl

1. Preheat oven to 450°F (230°C). Lightly oil a 16-inch (40-cm) pizza pan.

2. In a large bowl combine polenta with the cold water, then add the boiling water in a steady stream, mixing with a whisk. Stir in eggs and mozzarella cheese. Press mixture evenly onto pan. Bake until lightly browned and crisp (10–15 minutes).

3. In a large skillet over medium-high heat, sauté green onions in 2 tablespoons olive oil for 1 minute, then add bell pepper and mushrooms. Cover and let steam for 5 minutes.

4. Spoon sauce over cornmeal crust, then top with sautéed vegetables, sliced tomatoes, parsley, and basil. Bake until topping is bubbly (12–15 minutes).

Makes one 16-inch (40-cm) pizza.

Pizza Desserts

For pizza lovers, the perfect follow-up to a memorable pizza is one last luscious slice. Here's how to grant aficionados their fondest wish: Serve them pizza for dessert. In this section is a gala assortment of just-for-fun "fake" pizzas—easy-to-make treats you bake in pizza pans and decorate to look like the real thing.

TRIPLE-CHOCOLATE BROWNIE PIZZA

The mock pizza shown in the photograph combines peanut-butter and mocha ice creams but you can pick your own pair of favorite flavors.

as needed	butter or oil	as needed
1 lb	semisweet chocolate, chopped	450 g
¼ cup	unsweetened cocoa powder	60 ml
4 tbl	unsalted butter	4 tbl
5	eggs	5
1½ cups	sugar	350 ml
1½ tsp	vanilla extract	1½ tsp
1 cup	sifted flour	250 ml
½ tsp	baking powder	½ tsp
pinch	salt	pinch
8 oz each	chocolate chips and chopped walnuts	225 g each
1 qt each	vanilla and chocolate ice cream	900 ml
1 jar	bottled chocolate sauce (optional)	1 jar
as needed	assorted dessert toppings (optional)	as needed

1. Preheat oven to 350°F (175°C). Generously coat a 16-inch-diameter (40-cm) pizza pan with butter or oil.

2. In a saucepan over low heat, melt semisweet chocolate, cocoa, and 4 tablespoons butter, stirring until smooth. Remove from heat and let mixture cool about 5 minutes.

3. In a large bowl beat eggs and sugar with an electric mixer until thick and pale. Stir in vanilla and cooled chocolate mixture; blend well and set aside.

4. Combine flour, baking powder, and salt. Add to chocolate mixture, stirring just to combine. Fold in chocolate chips and nuts. Spread mixture in prepared pizza pan. Bake 30 minutes, then remove from oven. Meanwhile, remove vanilla ice cream from freezer to soften. Spread pizza with softened vanilla ice cream and dot with scoops of chocolate ice cream. Serve with chocolate sauce and various toppings, if desired.

Makes one 16-inch (40-cm) brownie pizza.

PIZZA GALETTE

A sweet flatbread of French origin is this big, buttery, sugar-crusted galette from the walled medieval city of Pérouges, near Lyon.

¾ cup	butter	175 ml
1 pkg (1 tbl)	active dry yeast	1 pkg (1 tbl)
¼ cup	warm water (about 105°F or 41°C)	60 ml
½ cup	sugar	125 ml
1 tsp	lemon zest	1 tsp
1	egg	1
⅛ tsp	salt	⅛ tsp
1¾ cups	flour	425 ml
as needed	oil	as needed

1. Soften ½ cup (125 ml) of the butter and set aside.

2. Sprinkle yeast over the water in a small bowl. Add 1 tablespoon of the sugar. Let stand until yeast is soft (about 5 minutes).

3. In large bowl of electric mixer, cream the ½ cup (125 ml) softened butter with 2 tablespoons of sugar until fluffy; blend in lemon zest, then egg. Stir salt into yeast mixture; blend into butter mixture. Gradually blend in flour to make a soft dough. Continue beating until dough is smooth and elastic (about 5 minutes).

4. Place dough in a greased bowl. Cover with plastic wrap and let rise in a warm place until doubled in bulk (about 1½ hours). Stir dough down.

5. Preheat oven to 425°F (220°C). Roll dough on a well-floured surface into a circle about 12 inches (30 cm) in diameter. Oil a 16-inch (40-cm) pizza pan. Pat and stretch dough to fit pan. Press into pan, pinching edge of dough to make a slightly raised rim. Cut the remaining ¼ cup (60 ml) butter into 24 equal pieces; distribute evenly over dough. Sprinkle with the remaining 5 tablespoons sugar. Bake until well browned (12–15 minutes). Cut into wedges and serve warm.

Makes one 16-inch (40-cm) flatbread.

Chocolate-Cherry Cookie Pizza

This giant, sugar-dusted pizza is perfect for boxing up carefully and mailing to a hungry college student or anyone else who appreciates a big chocolate chip cookie.

as needed	butter or oil	as needed
½ cup	butter, softened	125 ml
½ cup	firmly packed brown sugar	125 ml
1 tsp	vanilla extract	1 tsp
1 cup	flour	250 ml
1 cup	coarsely chopped semisweet chocolate	250 ml
½ cup	coarsely chopped pecans	125 ml
⅓ cup	red candied cherries, halved	85 ml
as needed	confectioners' sugar	as needed

1. Preheat oven to 375°F (190°C). Generously coat a 12-inch-diameter (30-cm) pizza pan with butter or oil.

2. In large mixer bowl beat butter and brown sugar until light and fluffy; blend in vanilla. Gradually add flour, mixing until blended. Stir in chocolate, pecans, and cherries.

3. Pat mixture evenly over surface of prepared pizza pan (dough will be thick; use your fingers to spread the dough evenly, if necessary), to within ¼ inch (.6 cm) of outer edge of pan.

4. Bake until well-browned (14–16 minutes). Cool for 10 minutes in pan on wire rack. Use a pizza cutter or knife to cut into wedges or leave whole. Sprinkle lightly with confectioners' sugar. Remove from pan when cool.

Makes one 12-inch (30-cm) cookie pizza.

ALMOND-RASPBERRY ICE CREAM PIZZA

This whimsical pizza is a cinch to prepare. Pick your favorite berry flavor—strawberry, raspberry, or blueberry—for the syrup and ice cream.

as needed	butter or oil	as needed
10 oz	slivered almonds, finely chopped	285 g
1 cup	unsalted butter, at room temperature	250 ml
⅓ cup	sugar	85 ml
2½ cups	flour	600 ml
1	egg, lightly beaten	1
1 tsp	almond extract	1 tsp
½ tsp	vanilla extract	½ tsp
⅛ tsp	salt	⅛ tsp
1 jar	bottled berry syrup	1 jar
1 qt	berry ice cream	900 ml
1 cup	almonds, chopped and toasted	250 ml

1. Preheat oven to 375°F (190°C). Generously coat a 16-inch-diameter (40-cm) pizza pan with butter or oil.

2. Combine slivered almonds, butter, sugar, flour, egg, almond and vanilla extracts, and salt. Mix well.

3. Press dough evenly into pan, leaving a ¼-inch (.6-cm) border around edge to allow crust to expand while baking. Chill at least 30 minutes in refrigerator or 15 minutes in freezer.

4. Remove crust from refrigerator or freezer and bake until crust is golden brown (about 20 minutes). Let cool.

5. With a spatula spread berry syrup over cooled crust. Top with small scoops of berry ice cream, covering entire surface. Sprinkle chopped, toasted nuts over ice cream and serve at once.

Makes one 16-inch (40-cm) cookie pizza.

Index